Blue Toes
and a Dog

Blue Toes and a Dog

a book of poetry by

Rudy Baron

PALMETTO
PUBLISHING
Charleston, SC
www.PalmettoPublishing.com

Paperback ISBN: 979-8-8229-5597-4

Thanks to Barbara Henning, M.L. Liebler, Lewis Warsh, Kenneth Bernard, and Wayne Berninger for their friendship and guidance.

Bill and Tracy (and their dog, Everton) for making me smile.

My daughters Julia and Kiki for their never-ending love and for making me feel young.

And a special thanks to Nina, for always believing in me. I miss her.

Edited by Will Randazzo

Art by Kiki Baron

Contents

It was hot today

but tonight ahead of showers
the wind is cool
floats by as giant
sympatico in memoriam
of wispy thoughts
I have missed

The ant that crossed my path
has disappeared
found its way into the neighbor's
living room
Into their kitchen
Into their stereo
Into their bathroom
the ant is now the tenant

I am glad they have returned
they have form and personality
individual character
reminders of friendly company
bar stools and blemished floors

And I want to know Mr. Ant
and his family
they are now neighbors
and when all this happened
you crossed your eyes

You said ants cannot be neighbors
You said don't be ridiculous
You said ants are ridiculous
You said I could never
be an ant
I crawl alone
on strained floors.

If the sun could smile
I could sit and stare
and wave
saying "hello," waiting
for a wave back
I will keep waving
and

Continue to watch

Rudy Baron

I don't like

Poetry
anymore
it doesn't seem to satisfy
my needs
straddle a sensitive fence
balance and juggle
look down in perpetual fear
at alligator moat filled
words
anxiously await approval

In letters
can I be read
someone please tell me
what those images on the cave wall
actually mean

Will they look back
will they respond in a chorus
of hallelujahs
will they bury themselves in
selfish states of simplistic
mediocrity
will I be healed—

I write blankly
coil behind a dark curtain
of closed eyelids
wait for some majestic painting
to unfold

Vivid expression, my emotions
that stain my shirt
bleeds from left
to right
its novel state
an island
floats along

Tapestry of skeleton
my bones woven cloth
complex strands of thread
appeared one day
suddenly burdened with the task
to watch vigilantly
over sterile fields

I'm sorry I said those things
I apologize for my meandering
excuse me for spontaneous oral eruptions
pardon that verbal misgiving
forgive that last moment we were together

Rudy Baron

I want to do something
I want to do something
for you
I want to explain
the taste of tomatoes
and the taste of your tongue
I want to lick the lines
of your hand
swallow the fortune
of your
future

Will I wander back
into useful language
should I tell friends
appropriate
notes of encouragement
hoping that last salutation
will suffice for a sign off

Or should I heroically
wave at ships
that have left the pier
succumb to previously
heard vibrations

I want

The rest of my life
to be
one
long
Fuck!

"It's difficult
to ar-tic-U-late,"
I explained
my life pressing
into darkness

"It's hard,"
I ges-tic-U-la-ted
squirming
enjoyably
eventually
leisurely
shrinking into

Com-for-TA-bil-i-ty

Isn't this a pause?
Isn't this a gap?
Isn't this time
to wait for a jolt?

Rudy Baron

A blip
on the radar
A speed bump
in a parking lot
A gust of wind
on the beach

I can only
wake for so long
before the morning
mendacity
of alarms
and voices
launches me
into a disruption

Can I differentiate
struggle
from satisfaction
perhaps eventually
easing
into a convenient
fold

Metaphors
allegories
analogies
and a subsequent rise

Only to deflate
into a concise
distinguished
explanation

Ignoring me
she stares
stone-faced
into her cup
of tepid
cappuccino

Lines

The craft show in the park guarantees it will rain this weekend,
dog limping on sunbaked slate sidewalk, water becomes a valuable
commodity on days of premature summer; let's arrange our children in
order by height, cower under a shroud of leaves.

The last conversation has been reduced to subdued discourse, a gardener
collects an array of cacophonous sounds, on an arid cheek a tear is
stranded, her fever eclipsed one hundred last night, the sound of beeping
signals the end of an event, crowds head for tents ahead of the rumbling
thunder.

I think I'll dress my child in stripes today, watch her skip over horizontal
cracks and explain why pavement is black; maybe she will pause for a
moment and stare at my perplexed view; maybe she will stare at my
perplexed view and question its existence; maybe she will stare at me and
question my existence; maybe she will stare and question whether my
existence necessitates a perplexed view.

The rain falls tonight in seemingly straight lines. It is cold and wet. If I
stood in the rain I would stand straight. My arms would be stretched out
above me, they would reach the lines of rain, they would be cold and wet,
and they would reach toward the sky.

Tonight, discussion is pressed keys. Letters are touched and caressed,
aren't they? Can we discuss our possessions in caressed moments
of touched words? Touched letters? Can we sell them simply by
description? Can we sell our lives by simply describing them in simple
phrases? Six feet tall—loves poetry—likes blue jeans—is old and fading.
Will you spread your life on my body like a classified ad on a naked
newspaper?

I want to talk in lines. I want to be seen like ridges in a desert. I want
ridges on a desert to explain me. I want the desert winds to create my
lines. I want my lines to create desert winds.

A leaf

Occupies my parking space
Does it know I'm arriving
The clouds roll in
I draw clouds
on paper towels
that melt when wet

One day I will be a cloud
One day I will cross the sky
One day I will block the sun
One day I will cross the ocean
casting a shadow on waters
One day I will sit above
and smile
One day I will collapse
into a morning shower

Do you mind
Do you mind my writing
Do you mind as I scribble
my jabbering chatter
of sun trees and clouds
Do you mind that I sit
beneath the universe
Do you mind that whispers
may be angry expressions

Rudy Baron

Can I wave like a tree
in the distance
side-to-side

Undecided and ambivalent
Unknown and irrelevant

Walks and talks
occupies
a fully furnished
living room
in my home

Dictates how feet move
Dictates whether to talk
or grit teeth
in discontent

Look at floating clouds
they are friends
arriving at a party
I am going to host

I can work the room
float through characters
while the cloud
becomes shapes
larger than
ice cream vistas

And that last group
had
A conversation
A conversation
A conversation
Another conversation
lost all fluffy
soaked with moisture
has disappeared
found its way onto
some neighboring floor
Into the kitchen
Into the bathroom
Into the bedroom
Into an occupant

When all this happened
don't be silly
it can't be silly

Seymour

Liked forming
the shape of a pretzel
bones snapping and cracking
unwinding from his twisted manner

The view from the window
is blocked by a building
absorbing the sun's rays
dripping them onto the sidewalk
silhouettes of crippled shadows

The library's books all contain
identical creases in the spine
patrons opening
to the same page

The exit over the doorway walks by
a blonde woman
watches the red second hand
pause for one second

Vacationers watch TV
on the beach
fluorescent light washes
away figures on the screen

Rudy Baron

If Seymour had an opinion
regarding all this
he would let it be known
through verbal ejaculations
or the thunderous tension
of premeditated silence

Seymour offers her a drink
she stares into the glass
listening to rumblings
restless
agitated ice cubes

Someone drives their heel
into a neighboring toe
screams some
visceral curse
thinking this is a step
in some form of direction

The air only gets heavy
when the sky ducks behind a cloud
a man with an ugly tie
discusses his breakfast

Seymour contemplates his existence
as a superhero
while thumbing his day through
shirts purchased at second hand stores

The name Slimey, the wet snail
has been co-opted by a small child
resistant to friendship and acts
of recognizable kindness
by wrinkled relatives

She can't dance! Never could!
the last line of a job evaluation
puts to rest any chance
of upward mobility

Seymour
acknowledges
the eyes close
the curtain opens to dream
the knock of familiarity

Tentatively explaining long paragraphs

the day the hour the tobacco shop

a time of inventory visible streets letter of the alphabet
        a "P" signifying "parking" outside hotel below the "P"

in another direction four carts carry vegetables in the
        opposite direction of a bus circling the plaza carrying
        a slogan

just a walk to the fountain or a church from my house by car
        carrying a loaf of bread

my mailman with the classic haircut underneath the sun
        cleaned nicely not made dirtier the German conductor
        red

blue bag blue taxi blue roads green shoes yogurt is dessert

a walk to the station in a northerly direction

the conductor carries a sack of potatoes and a stack of
        photographs

a man forms a pyramid out of pastries sells the street to
        the conductor while another conductor reproduces art
        during a moment of calm pauses

diverse seasons simultaneously years decades
        centuries stand in other positions dispense specific
        energies two discussions turn to three discussions
        forming a locomotion two or three turns of the wheel

tourists in public transport determine degrees of motivation
        waiting slowly to walk with past decisions positioned
        on foot page a taxi

the woman with the face of a tapestry lights a cigarette

three motorbikes enter the café and park beneath a calendar

the woman enters a church lacking fire she eats
        gelato with a loaf of bread in her hand selling mail to
        former bus occupants in line by order of privileges

they went into the road and joined the children playing in
        blue water proudly displaying a credit card
        taken from the man at the bar

two taxis at the taxi stand
        a young man posing with adamant security
        two men smoking a pipe carrying a dark purse

the woman wearing a simple jacket turns old

a group of people looking for parking send
    telegrams by bicycle

the baby with the dog holds a postcard displaying the blue ocean
    trots with him on his way to school

three taxis at the taxi stand

skeptical people in front of a church the road is orange a man wearing
a tie
    enters a funeral procession afterward
    enrolls in auto school

there are now five taxis waiting at the taxi stand

a death follows three babies to school
    another two acting green
    circling the circle stop

in front of the bus stop names dancing on lips
    are permanent smoke from a pipe
    smoked by a man carrying a dark purse

a baby in a baby car spreads a small rumor

at the bar passing through the door a woman with a purse
    leaves young men with designer postcards

passing a man with three roses watching veterans on foot
    in the middle of the street

Rudy Baron

what causes this movement at the same time
        not an external reading nor particular motivations

at the bus stop forty men and two children arrive explaining
        the road the fire the baby with the dog
        the man in the pullover screaming

the coroner for all churches awakes at 2:30

the old man with green hands flags down a bus
        possibly pretending to be seventy living outside a mortuary
        late for a 2:45 picnic

* * *

Very late enter the tobacco bar saluting the only piano
        hotly occupied by a man who generally plays
        bridge on the fourth day of every month

he decides he will sit at the table in the morning
        eat his meal and drink his wine

a bicycle a motorcycle a mail truck a school bus a beautiful
        woman have already stopped at the restaurant

grandmothers out for a walk present a gift to the
        proprietor of the bar who goes for rides
        with his clients

the conductor stops in the front of the tobacco bar to play
　　　bridge for the first time through an open window

a motorcyclist finds aerodynamics imperative at the same
　　　moment the mailman rides by carrying letters lacking
　　　addresses with thoughts of where to drop them off

someone more or less reading a letter written on green
　　　paper pauses briefly interested in a telescope
　　　a baby who makes walking motions dressed
　　　in a suit the color of eggplants

a policeman with two dogs that are related
　　　a man holding a scale
　　　a man painting asterisks
　　　on mailboxes for lost letters

the hat of a man arrives on foot

a woman with a loaf of bread wants to change the music
　　　reads the newspaper outside
　　　the abandoned newspaper stand

notice some book seen in an antique store
　　　warm days always come in pairs
　　　enter and sit at an open window

the first hour passes loudly the second much quieter
　　　to rest is improbable
　　　another man carries a sack with an initial on it

Rudy Baron

a blue car a car the color of honeydews
        a glass of beer the color of coffee

the "P" for "parking" is now illuminated diverse offices
        all illuminated are visible

the third hour passes patiently

a door opens a taxi becomes illuminated stops in front of a theater
        people in red and blue hats communicate
        helplessly alone

children play under church lights taking half-steps
        beside a beautifully illuminated dog

a client rises to leave offering to pay another time another man
        wants to enter the bar must dance with the client

outside a man sings the same carol twice
        turning verses into incantations

outside someone watches with a distinguished face

outside the color of fire is rare elucidation

outside a policeman is on his way to church

outside somber winds are machine made

outside it is night and summer waits to pass

outside the day never protests its routine

a man the age of retirement carries a tapestry
   traffic continues going straight

a man passes carrying a coronet

a man passes carrying a small table

a man passes carrying a plastic sculpture not noticing
   what else he may carry

a man leaves behind a letter contentedly deciding
   to pick it up later

evening enters the window

the pavement imitates the sky during a storm

Rudy Baron

Julia says...

(a poem cowritten by my daughter, who was seven at the time)

Alligator is green and long
munching on mostly unsuspecting creatures
that wander too close
what is he thinking
when he smiles that grin

She's lost six teeth she claims
not really
yanked out by a dentist
with the straightest, whitest
does he practice on himself
squirting that gum numbing liquid

Mouths are big black holes
wide, swallowing everything in sight
flowers, animals
ouch, it would hurt
if you swallowed a bee

The boy with the big head
one day swallowed an entire hive
his father put up a sign
sold tickets to eager viewers

This craziness is weird because
it's like madness and they're almost the same
except craziness starts with a "C"
and madness doesn't

Words don't mind occupying the same space
even if they come from the same family
with utterly distinct personalities
one with the eyes of an angel fish
who's lived beyond his years

She is eight
but if she were one hundred
she would say, "Here comes a sickness
Blah, I'm dead"

The boy with the bad braces
picks up Russian radio and swears
there are strangers arriving soon

Old women cackling over
boiling cauldrons of goulash
gossip about unloved relatives
in foreign lands and never heard from

In the water
looking out over the horizon thinking
until that truck roared by
blowing dust and sand
deafening sounds surround the sky

Dead rabbits, a struck deer
clouds are white mustaches
swimming

A most sincere looking toad
winked and leapt upon a shoulder
whispered a secret he wasn't a toad at all
rather the former cook
of a fine dining establishment

Fired when someone ate
bad deviled eggs
tasted like they had frog spawn in them
Yep, you heard that right
frog spawn

"Alice!" the note said
Why would Alice be writing
when it was the Queen that burped

These offerings should not be confused
with unfounded rumors of waterbeds
filled with multicolored goldfish
squishing beneath as you sleep

It's bedtime tired, snuggled
in, under the covers
almost forgot
to include the stuffed animals

They invaded the bed
a safari, shooting bubbles
capturing baby tigers floating
over the jungle

Big and wide and running around
all over the place

They are green and blue
and everyone's hair is purple

"How can you get so...?"

Popcorn

Popcorn is yellow
or is it white
"I don't quite remember,"
she cried
If you do, call
If you don't, call anyone

Have you got a dime?
I'll ask the man in the purple
pajamas and fuzzy slippers
He smiles and winks
shows me a quarter
requires I do a magic trick

Johnny!
It was sprinkles on my cheerleading
pom-poms this time
I wish mom would leave him
in the yard, so mean
crime and slime
all is grime
la la la la

Can I stop singing?
No!
Can I stop saying la?
la la la la
OK, now?
No! Never!

Rudy Baron

Nigel snarls at doctors
doesn't like them
feeling the pain of probing
arthritic vertebrae

"They're going to cure you"
his wife yells from a 3rd floor fire escape
The only question she ever asked
was "What's wrong?"

The blinds at the corner tailor
are too short
a great temptation
for zealous, rampant peeping Toms
the line goes around the corner
begins at the newspaper stand
where children
sell overpriced lemonade

Can you follow up with that?
Can you get back to me?
Can you please repeat every word
I've ever spoken?
Can you please tell me
exactly what I mean?
Can you move aside?
Can you please let me through?

I'll have a cup of coffee
apologize for an early departure
the TV remote is dead
and my eyes don't dance anymore
A flickering shadow
trees tangoing in moonlight
fading music of the wind

This summer has seen a rise in shells
washed up on the beach
elderly men pay boys
to throw them back
hoping to slow the tides
and the erosion of time

The next morning

The first thing she said,
"Your dick is too big"

How does one respond
to such a greeting?
Explain to me
this exclamation
What makes my dick
bigger than his
or his
or his?

Are there classifications for dicks;
have, unbeknownst to me,
they been secretly measured
and cataloged by size,
mine listed somewhere
between normal
and enormous.

Possibly there are volumes
of Baron dicks
detailed and dated,
sepia toned
vintage photography
tracing my ancestral
dick lineage.

Or consider the many
gym lockers I've frequented
surrounded by an immeasurable
number of dicks
in assorted
shapes and sizes
acting either shy and bashful
or boasting its proud
protuberant prominence

Maybe they are
like wrinkles
or snowflakes
no two are the same
the dick diversity
incredibly increasing daily

Should I reach down
and cup the package
consider its mass
in proportion to
other "too big" objects
elephants, whales,
the universe?

Or perhaps I should
resign myself to
her proclamation
simply address my
seemingly uber-standard staff
like a friendly puppy dog
happily going for a walk
"Who's the big fella?
Who's the big fella?
You are, aren't you?
Yes,
You are!"

The past year

I'm adjusting
I'm adjusting!
I'm adjusting?

I'm learning to adjust
this past year

Not entirely sure
what all of that means

I'm adjusting to
the phrase "Moving on to the next chapter"
while still working on the prologue

I'm adjusting to
sobering dreams
and soapy mornings

I'm adjusting to
my belly button evolving
from an innie to an outie

I'm adjusting to
the silence of children's feet
ghosts of age

I'm adjusting to
memory—my mother's last breath
"I love you, too"

I'm adjusting to
a liver removed
from a comatose girl
a dull Saturday night

I'm adjusting to
a smirk carved
on my belly
with tits for eyes

I'm adjusting to
a face
the morning mirror
reflects a new wrinkle

I'm adjusting to
collected souvenirs
decaying homeless
figments of the mind

I'm adjusting to
the page and ink
soiling the floor

I'm adjusting to
Mortality
contemplating raindrops
that collapse
during a storm

I'm adjusting to
to the sweetness of existence
the security of repetition

I'm adjusting to
happiness and pain
regardless of
the morning sun

Blue toes

The dog despised
FedEx
violently barking as
trucks pass the window

With menace
protects his food
beneath a shag rug
hiding a coffee stain

He has become
accustomed to stale
mornings
watching flowers open
in stop motion animation

She shows she cares
through anger
insisting it
makes him special

Damp-eyed
collecting
the dinner table
remains
a feeble feast

Common truths
are necessary antidotes
to muttered lies

Sometimes
hurricanes and tornadoes
are better than
clear skies
and sunshine

And sometimes
life's calm
is replaced with
gravel roads
and potholes

Puddles of melted snow
driven over
until they dry up
and disappear

Chloe

C-H-L-O
Chlo
sparkling star
in the stillness
of my dreams

I
C-H-L-Ohhh
breath your soul
at night
Chlo
and melt
irresistibly
in your eyes

C is for caress
and Hold your
shape Loving you
intertwined Our
bodies collapsing
into a clear pool

Chlo
I want to swim
in the ocean
that surrounds you
drinking
your waters

C-H-L-O
Chlo
a whisper
a song
a puff
perfumed air
forming
a gentle cloud

Cccchhhhllllloooo
Elongated
Enunciated
Everlasting
Sublime echo
of your name

C-H-L-O
Chlo
I want to taste
each letter
on your lips
individually
consonants
and vowel

C—-H—-L—-O

Forestlawn

Rectangular mirror over the dresser
ceramic elephant ashtrays
painting of three dogs
a card table
men at the dining table
playing poker
throwing coins
rubbing green felt

mother waters tulips
I pull a petal off
try to separate the colors
white and black tiled
kitchen floor
gray stairs to the basement
a rusty push mower
rests under
the front porch

she tells me if I cry in church
they will cut off my
head
I turn in the pew
a woman carries a headless child
through the door

Five p.m.—father home
his black
lunchbox
soiled work shoes
my lips
against his sandpaper cheek

after kissing my first girl
I didn't get any milk
or saltine crackers
I hated them anyways

Uncle Pete smokes Lucky Strikes
sits in a turtle-waxed
Detroit River Lazy-Boy
my eyes drawn
tomato vines
the backyard
aromas from the kitchen

my head on mother's lap
an Italian lullaby
sung for no one else

Virginia,

(d.1941)

What are those worms
eating your words
away your mind
what are they confessing
in your subconscious tomb

Laborious words
passing through a sieve
separated strands
detached from their brethren
spilling a straight strain
the heart shreds
itself into minuscules
of disconnected clarity
collecting on the floor
cold cracked ice
fogged view below your feet
what do you see
under the ice, Virginia

Are the storms beneath you
standing
waiting
to be talked
from the edge of the cliff

staring at strewn bodies
amongst the rocks below
bobbing bobbles
that mockingly smile
only when the tide
rolls them over

Rudy Baron

Dawn

Taste the popsicle blue
of the sky
and the buttery yellow
of the sun

I've knelt at various
alters and common
wishing wells
tossing coins
into the kitty

I believe
I'm supposed to love you
for more than
one night

Isn't that the idea
Isn't that the concept
Isn't that the requirement

Children with sharp sticks
chase pigeons
on museum steps
scattering
shrieking
in gleeful terror

The decaying body
of a dead bird
fills the creases of a
cloudy sidewalk

I could reach out
grab cotton candy
clouds
stuff them into
my mouth
eat the sky
let it all dissolve

I can taste the life of clouds
imagine the beauty
of floating

Can I talk about pain
and comfort and you
and love and conversation
and listening and whispering
of ears and lips
voices and hands
clenched tightly together
into one erotic
coiling fist

Rudy Baron

Please tell me the purpose
of my life
why do I resemble a character
in your fictional existence
who am I in your cryptic
babble, babble, and dribble

I think I will pull a branch
taste the leaves
and taste their lives
how sweet they exist
one day I will listen to
the wind
if I listen enough
I will understand

Milton Keynes UK
Ingram Content Group UK Ltd.
UKHW030002260824
447288UK00004B/201